ANDY RILEY IS THE AUTHOR/ARTIST OF
**THE BOOK OF BUNNY SUICIDES, RETURN OF THE BUNNY SUICIDES,
GREAT LIES TO TELL SMALL KIDS, LOADS MORE LIES TO
TELL SMALL KIDS** AND **THE BUMPER BOOK OF BUNNY
SUICIDES.** HIS WEEKLY CARTOON STRIP, **ROASTED,** RUNS IN THE
OBSERVER MAGAZINE AND IS ALSO COMPILED AS A HODDER
AND STOUGHTON HARDBACK.

HIS SCRIPTWRITING WORK INCLUDES **BLACK BOOKS, HYPERDRIVE,
LITTLE BRITAIN, SLACKER CATS, SMACK THE PONY, BIG
TRAIN, THE ARMANDO IANNUCCI SHOWS, SPITTING IMAGE,
THE ARMSTRONG AND MILLER SHOW, THE FRIDAY NIGHT
ARMISTICE, SO GRAHAM NORTON, THE 99p CHALLENGE,**
AND THE BAFTA-WINNING ANIMATION **ROBBIE THE REINDEER.**

D.I.Y. DENTISTRY

...AND OTHER ALARMING INVENTIONS

ANDY RILEY

HODDER &
STOUGHTON

FIRST PUBLISHED IN GREAT BRITAIN BY HODDER & STOUGHTON
A HACHETTE LIVRE UK COMPANY

1 3 5 7 9 10 8 6 4 2

A CIP CATALOGUE RECORD FOR THIS TITLE IS AVAILABLE FROM
THE BRITISH LIBRARY.

ISBN 9 780340 899656

PRINTED AND BOUND BY WILLIAM CLOWES LTD.

HODDER & STOUGHTON POLICY IS TO USE PAPERS THAT ARE
NATURAL, RENEWABLE AND RECYCLABLE PRODUCTS AND MADE
FROM WOOD GROWN IN SUSTAINABLE FORESTS, THE LOGGING
AND MANUFACTURING PROCESSES ARE EXPECTED TO CONFORM TO
THE ENVIRONMENTAL REGULATIONS OF THE COUNTRY OF ORIGIN.

HODDER & STOUGHTON LTD.
338 EUSTON RD.
LONDON NW1 3BH
WWW. HODDER. CO. UK

WITH THANKS TO:

POLLY FABER, CAMILLA HORNBY,
BEN DUNN, ELENI FOSTIROPOULOS,
EVERYONE ELSE AT HODDER,
KEVIN CECIL, FELICITY BLUNT, FREYA AYRES

AND

W. HEATH ROBINSON
WILF LUNN

SELF-BURYING COFFIN

WORLD'S CHEAPEST HAIRDRYER

A METHOD FOR FISH
WHO WANT TO EVEN
THINGS UP A BIT

'POLE-DANCING-CLUB-IN-A-BRIEFCASE' FOR THE STRANDED BUSINESSMAN

ALL-TERRAIN POGO STICK ASSAULT FORCE

'STRAIGHT FROM THE COW' MILK SHAKES

THE
'SNOTWRITER'
FOUNTAIN PEN

—NEVER RUNS OUT

THE
ARSEHOLE TRAP

CLEARS AN AVERAGE-SIZED
TOWN OF ARSEHOLES IN JUST
A *SINGLE DAY*

GLITTERBALLS
FOR GOTH
NIGHTCLUBS

CHOPSTICK HEAVY LIFTER
FOR CHINESE BUILDING SITES

FOUR-WAY FOOTBALL

— DECIDES A WORLD CUP GROUP IN A SINGLE AFTERNOON

36-WAY FOOTBALL

— DECIDES THE *ENTIRE WORLD CUP* IN A SINGLE AFTERNOON

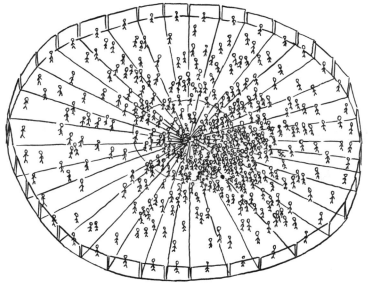

THE PIZZA LEAFLET INSTANT DISPOSAL SYSTEM

WATERPROOF SUIT ENABLING THIRSTY
HIKERS TO DRINK THEIR OWN SWEAT

SYSTEM #1 FOR THE SWIFT PROCESSING OF MOPED THIEVES

WASHING LINES FOR VIKINGS

SYSTEM FOR BEATING TRAFFIC JAMS

SUBBUTEO CHESS

APPARATUS FOR CROSSING MOTORWAYS SAFELY ON FOOT

THE Nagpod™

- PERFECT FOR ADJUSTING SPOUSE'S BEHAVIOUR
- PROGRAMMABLE WITH OVER 10,000 INSTRUCTIONS, WARNINGS AND HELPFUL ADMONITIONS
- SELECT "SHUFFLE" FOR RANDOM NAGS

AUTO — SCOOPER FOR DOGS

FLAVOURED GLACIERS

SYSTEM #2 FOR THE SWIFT PROCESSING OF MOPED THIEVES

METHOD FOR SHEEP TO DISGUISE THEMSELVES
AS SMALL FLUFFY CLOUDS WHEN THREATENED
BY A WOLF

THE
TOASTER-LAPTOP
FOR CONVENIENT SURFING 'N' SNACKING

AUTOMATIC TREE-PLANTING HUMMER
FOR GUILT-FREE 4 × 4 MOTORING

SURVEILLANCE BAUBLES

—TELL SANTA IF YOU'VE BEEN BAD OR GOOD
INSTANTLY

MOEBIUS STRIP MAPS FOR HIKERS WHO
ENJOY AN INTELLECTUAL CHALLENGE

UNICORN STORAGE RACK

'COP CATAPULT' FOR RAPID RESPONSE TO URBAN CRIME

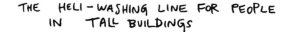

THE HELI-WASHING LINE FOR PEOPLE
   IN   TALL BUILDINGS

CAMEL IDENTIFYING MACHINE FOR THE BUSY ZOOKEEPER

A CALCULATOR FOR
PEOPLE WHO DON'T
LIKE NUMBERS
BIGGER THAN FOUR

THE MACH CENTURY™

- THE WORLD'S FIRST ONE HUNDRED BLADE RAZOR

- MORE BLADES MEANS THE CLOSEST SHAVE **EVER**

BEFORE

AFTER

THE ROBOTIC BURGER BUGGY

WON'T LET ITSELF BE
CAUGHT UNTIL YOU'VE
JOGGED OFF ALL THE
CALORIES YOU'RE ABOUT
TO EAT

CHEAP AIR TRAVEL

YO! SUSHI VARIANTS

PORTABLE
YO! SUSHI FOR
MUSIC FESTIVALS

DIVERSIFYING:
YO! HARDWARE

YO! STUNT SUSHI

A WEB INTERFACE ESPECIALLY FOR PIGS

TREADLE-POWERED
BELLY BUTTON
DE-FLUFFER

STEAM
BATH
FOR
A PET
MOUSE

ENFORCING "GIVE WAY" SIGNS

THE
"VIOLINVIOLACELLOBASS"
AN ENTIRE STRING QUARTET IN ONE HANDY INSTRUMENT

baby transport

SHELL-POOLING LANES FOR SNAILS

BUSINESS CLASS EXECUTIONS
FOR LAW-BREAKING C.E.O.s

'CADDY TROUSERS' FOR GOLFERS

HALLOWEEN FUN

NOVELTY HALLOWEEN KEBAB MEAT

WITH EMBEDDED PLASTIC HUMAN SKULLS AND PELVISES

PUMPKIN LASER LANTERN
EMITS A WELCOMING ORANGE GLOW WHICH BURNS THROUGH TRICK-OR-TREATERS IN $\frac{1}{8}$ OF A SECOND

'SCREAM'-THEMED URINALS

URBAN OVERCROWDING SOLVED:

CLIP-ON MINI-HOMES FOR YOUNG PROFESSIONALS

100% GUARANTEED WEIGHT LOSS METHOD

GUARANTEED 100% SUCCESSFUL
BINOCULARS FOR BIRDWATCHERS

OUTDOOR SMOKING TERRACE FOR THE A380 AIRBUS

SWISS ARMY GARDEN TOOL

KER-ZOOM

THE NEW BOARD GAME FOR 2-6 VERY IMPATIENT PLAYERS

DEVICE FOR GETTING SERVED FIRST AT THE BAR

CHEAP TECHNIQUE FOR HAIR EXTENSIONS

JUNIOR SATNAV

FOR LITTLE KID'S RIDES

MACHINE FOR GETTING THE REMOTE CONTROL
FROM THE OTHER END OF THE SOFA

folk tales

BEAR PORRIDGE
DEFENCE SYSTEM

WOLF/GRANDMOTHER
FACIAL RECOGNITION
SOFTWARE

NEGATIVE
MATCH

ANTI
CLIMB
PAINT

JACK-
PROOFED
BEANSTALK

STAY IN TOUCH
AND STAY NEAT
WITH

SHAVERPHONE

TOUR DE FRANCE
WITHOUT LEAVING
YOUR OWN BEDROOM

"SLIP-ON" IRONS FOR HANDS-FREE DE-WRINKLING

ROTARY NOSE PICKER

- GOES CLOCKWISE OR ANTICLOCKWISE
- COMES WITH 30-PIECE SET OF DIFFERENT SIZED INDEX FINGERS

HUSBAND PUB SESSION TERMINATION SYSTEM

GUARANTEED WAKE UP SYSTEM FOR PEOPLE WITH NASAL PIERCINGS

CAMPERVAN SKATEBOARD

GREEN POWER

COMPULSORY WIND
FARM HATS FOR
TALL PEOPLE

HYDRO-
ELECTRIC
URINAL
POWER
STATION

ENDLESS LIGHT
BULB

SOLAR CELLS
POWER LIGHT BULB
WHICH SHINES ON
SOLAR CELLS WHICH
POWER LIGHT BULB
WHICH SHINES ON
SOLAR CELLS WHICH
POWERS LIGHT BULB
WHICH.... (ETC.)

FROG NEUTRALISATION SYSTEM
FOR POND-DWELLING FLIES

BUNK DESKS

SAVING SPACE IN THE MODERN OFFICE

TUNGSTEN STEEL ANTI-MUGGING ARMOUR

THE GODZILLA EXPERIENCE (£20 FOR FIFTEEN MINUTES)

BOX OF 100 'MAN-SIZE'
DISPOSABLE DUVETS

SPORTS MADE EASY

'BIG HOLE' GOLF

ASSISTED DUNK

PRESS TO RISE

16-STUMP CRICKET WICKETS

FLY-BY-WIRE DARTS

INSTANT CYCLEPATH

PUPPYBOARDING

SOLITAIRE BOXING